THE PRO APPROACH

(FOR BECOMING A COMPLETE PLAYER)

BY: LARRY MATHEWS

INTRODUCTION

My name is Larry Mathews. I began bowling in 1962. I have been a member of the Professional Bowlers Association since 1975. I have won tournaments on a local, state, regional, and national level. In the thirty-three years I have been involved in the "Sport of Tenpins", I have had the privilege, and the pleasure, to coach some of the finest amateur and professional bowlers ever to "lace them up". Through the relationships and, more importantly, the friendships that were cultivated, I have grown as a person and as a teacher. Their names are far too numerous to mention; however, I want **them to know** that without their input, this endeavor would never have been possible.

While writing this manual, I am assuming that anyone who purchases it has a knowledge of the fundamentals of the sport. This is **not designed for the beginner**! It is written for the people that have taken their game to a certain level, and now find improvement to be next to impossible. Whether your average is 175 or 225, the information available, for your perusal, will enable you to take your game to the next level. The amount of success you experience is totally dependent upon your ability to understand and apply the premises set forth. Enjoyable reading and noticeable progress for you is my intent. I hope we both achieve our respective goals.

FOR MY WIFE, BARBARA.

TABLE OF CONTENTS

Chapter I:

PARALLEL LINES

In order to succeed in the sport of bowling, **you must understand the concept of** *Parallel Lines*. This term refers to the parallel configuration of the boards on the lane in relationship to the alignment you are attempting to play. In the Parallel Lines System, there are three *basic alignments* that can be utilized on any environment:

- **Parallel or Straight Up**
- **Swing**
- **Point**

(see the illustrations on page 2)

In order to mathematically determine any of these available **methods of attack**, you must be aware of your *base key*. Determining this number requires a knowledge of the following items:

- **Toe-to-shoulder distance**. This is merely the amount of space between your sliding shoe and your bowling shoulder (usually between 8 and 12 boards, based upon your physical make-up).

- **Drift pattern**. This is based upon your **starting position on the approach**, versus **where you slide**, when attempting to walk straight.

- **Perspective variable**. This refers to what you **hit**, versus what you **see**, while bowling (usually 1 to 2 boards inside your target).

I will now discuss how to properly determine each of the aforementioned configurations. Without a thorough understanding of these premises, it is very difficult to correctly set up any specific alignment.

Toe-to-shoulder distance. This (the measurement of the space between the center of the sliding shoe to the bowling shoulder) is determined by placing the center of your sliding shoe on the 20th board (middle dot), bringing your feet together, extending your arms to your side and locking your elbows, with your fingers **perpendicular** to the approach; then, **bend your knees** until the fingers of your bowling hand touch the approach (normally, board 9, 10, or 11). Compute the difference by subtracting the board that you touched from 20.

> Example: Standing on 20, my fingers touched 9; therefore, 20 - 9 = 11, which equals MY toe-to-shoulder distance.

Log this number. (For all future mathematical references, regarding the distance between toe and shoulder, I will use the number 10).

3 Basic Alignments

<table>
<tr><td>T = Target
A = Arc</td><td></td><td>Straight Up = Interaction
Point = Induced Hook
Swing = Induced Skid</td></tr>
</table>

Right-Handed Bowler

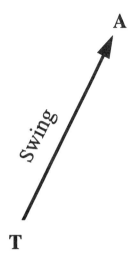

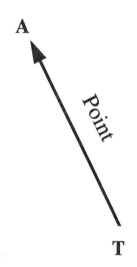

Left-Handed Bowler

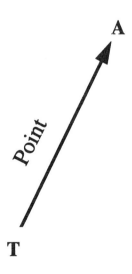

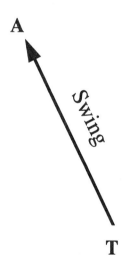

Straight Up Alignment = Break Point of 30'

Point Alignment = Break Point of 30' - 1.5' x (# Boards of Point)

Swing Alignment = Break Point of 30' + 1.5' x (# Boards of Swing)

Drift pattern. This is the most difficult of the three configurations to determine because of the inconsistency that exists in most bowlers approaches predicated upon the incorrect concept of always trying to walk toward your target, regardless of the alignment. I teach that you must try to walk straight, which will allow your drift to be dictated by the physiological imbalances each individual experiences when carrying a bowling ball to the foul line (in ninety percent of the players that I teach, the drift pattern is **always** in the opposite direction of the hand delivering the ball: right-handers drift left; left-handers drift right).

Determining your base key:
Take your toe-to-shoulder distance and add it to your target.

> Example: You are looking 10 and your toe-to-shoulder is 10; therefore, 10 + 10 = 20.

Then stand with the center of your sliding shoe on the 20th board, focusing on the 10th board on the lane. Try to walk as straight as you possibly can, reaching through your target and delivering the ball. Remain stationary at the point of release, turning your sliding shoe perpendicular to the foul line, notating where you slid. Repeat this procedure twenty to thirty times, or until a consistent drift pattern emerges. Notate the results!

> Example: Started 20, Slid 24 - A drift of 4 boards to the left; Started 20, Slid 18 - A drift of 2 boards to the right. A drift pattern to the left is a *minus factor*; therefore, a drift pattern to the right is a *plus factor* (for left-handers, the plus and minus factors are reversed).

Your base key may now be established by simply adding the plus or minus factor that your drift represents to your toe-to-shoulder distance.

> Example #1: A toe-to-shoulder of 10 boards plus a drift of 4 boards to the right equals a base key of 14 (10 + (+4) = 14).

> Example #2: A toe-to-shoulder of 10 boards plus a drift of 3 boards to the left equals a base key of 7 (10 + (-3) = 7).

Once you have determined your base key, your only other concern, on a mathematical basis, when attempting to compute any of the three basic alignments (parallel or straight up, swing, and point), is your perspective variable.

> **Note**: left-handers, please remember to transpose (drift left ($\leftarrow$) = plus factor; drift right ($\rightarrow$) = minus factor).

Perspective variable. This (what you SEE versus what you HIT) is an interesting phenomena and is relatively simple to determine. I suggest the following two methods for my students when attempting to ascertain a solution to this dilemma:

1. Have a fellow bowler, who is aware of this problem, watch you bowl, and then ask for his or her opinion.

2. Place a coin on the board you are attempting to hit; if you continually miss it, move it 1 or 2 boards to the inside. The placement of the coin, in reference to your target that you hit the most, out of 10 tries from every position utilized, will indicate to you your correct perspective variable.

You can expect a difference of 1 to 2 boards to the inside of your visual reference.

> Example: If your perspective variable is 1, when you target 10, you will hit 11.

Keep in mind that some bowlers hit where they look; some hit to the inside; a very few actually hit to the outside. Please relate to the fact that if you hit to the inside of your visual target, when determining your *look*, your perspective variable is a minus(-) factor.

> Example: You want to hit 12, so with a perspective variable of -2 (which indicates that you are hitting, on a great shot, exactly 2 boards to the inside of your visual target) you must look at 10 (12 - 2 = 10).

If you hit to the outside, your perspective variable is a plus (+) factor.

> Example: You want to hit 12, so with a perspective variable of +1 (which indicates that you are hitting, on a great shot, exactly 1 board to the outside of your visual target) you must look at 13 (12 + 1 = 13).

If you happen to be one of the select few that hit where they look, then your hit and look are one in the same; therefore, your perspective variable is 0.

> Example: You want to hit 12, and your perspective variable is 0 (which indicates that you are hitting, on a great shot, exactly where you look) so you must look at 12 (12 + 0 = 12).

Once you have determined your perspective variable, you have the last piece of necessary information that is needed to set up any alignment. Without this information, you will not be able to quickly line up off an opponent when that person is scoring and you are not. Obviously having this information at your disposal could create an advantage, and isn't **that** what reading this manual is all about? I will now give you some formulas that will make computing any desired alignment very easy.

- Approach position for parallel (straight up) = KEY + TARGET
- Approach position for a swing = KEY + TARGET + AMOUNT OF SWING
- Approach position for a point = KEY + TARGET − AMOUNT OF POINT

Remember, your **target**, in all computations, equals desired **hit** plus or minus your **perspective variable**.

When computing any of the three basic alignments, you must take into consideration what each entails when relating to the board you actually hit versus the **arc**.

- **Parallel (Straight Up)** — hit and arc are the **same** (hit 10, arc 10)
- **Swing** — arc is to the **outside** of the hit (hit 10, arc 8 = 2 board swing)
- **Point** — arc is to the **inside** of the hit (hit 10, arc 11 = 1 board point)

FORMULA FOR ALIGNMENT

Example: I want to play a 4 board swing, with my ball crossing the arrows at 10, and arcing 6. My key is 8 (toe-to-shoulder of 10, drift of 2 to the inside) and my perspective variable is (-1) (on a great shot, I hit 1 board **inside** of my target).

Step One.   I determine my visual target (look) which equals my perspective variable plus my desired hit. Therefore, my target, in order for me to hit 10, equals 9 (10 + (-1) = 9). My look or target is 9.

Step Two.   The answer to Step One, which is a target of 9, plus my key of 8, equals 9 + 8 which = 17. This determines my approach position in order to be playing a parallel alignment at 10. I would stand 17; drifting 2 to the inside, I would slide 19; my shoulder would then be in line with 9 (19 - 10 = 9); targeting 9, I would **hit** 10 and **arc** 10 because in a parallel alignment[1], your hit and your arc are the same (if I were intending to play straight up, my computation would be complete; however, in this example, I plan to play a 4 board swing. Therefore, one more computation is needed).

Step Three.   The answer to Step Two, which is an approach position of 17, plus for the amount of swing, or minus for the amount of point. In this particular situation, I'm attempting to play a 4 board swing, 10 to 6; therefore, I must take the straight up approach position of 17 and add 4 boards for the swing: 17 + 4 = 21.

The answer to Step One equals 9; answer to Step Two equals 17; answer to Step Three equals 21; therefore, **standing** 21, I'll **slide** 23 (2 board drift to the **inside**), **shoulder** at 13 (23 - 10), **target** 9, **hit** 10 (due to my perspective variable of 1), and, on a 4 board swing, **arc** at 6.

---

[1]For all future references, parallel alignment will be called "straight up" so as not to confuse an alignment with an adjustment.

The **formula for alignment**, once again, is this:

Step One.   **Look** versus **hit** = **hit** plus my perspective variable (P.V.) = **my target**.

Step Two.   **Answer to Step One** plus my **key** = **straight up** approach position.

Step Three.   **Answer to Step Two** plus for a swing; minus for a point = **final** approach position.

Let us continue with some mathematical examples, since the main advertisement for my teaching is for you to "Come to Larry Mathews, to learn to **use** the **math**." I truly believe that **success in the sport of bowling is based upon your ability to control the arc point**. Therefore, without a thorough knowledge of each component and formula previously discussed in this chapter, the aforementioned task is difficult, at best!

In all of the following examples, I will use a key of 8 (toe-to-shoulder of 10, with a drift of 2 to the inside [10 + (-2) = 8]), and a perspective variable (P.V.) of (-2) (I hit 2 boards **inside** my intended target on a great shot). I will use the Formula for Alignment that is on the previous page.

Note: If you implement a minus factor when determining your target, through utilization of your perspective variable (in order to hit 10, I must look 8 because I have a perspective variable of a (-2), so, 10 + (- 2) = 8), then you must implement a plus factor when determining what you hit (I'm looking 7 so I will hit 9 because 7 plus a perspective variable of (+2) equals 9. Keep this in mind when viewing the examples below.)

Example #1: My desired alignment is to hit 9 on a 5 board swing, arcing 4 (break point).

Step One: Visual Target = 9 + perspective variable of (-2) = 7 = **look**

Step Two: Answer to Step One = **look** of 7 + **key** (8) = 15 = approach position straight up

Step Three: Answer to Step Two = 15 + swing of 5 boards = 20 = final approach position

Solution: Stand 20, Slide 22, Shoulder at 12, Look 7, Hit 9, Arc 4 (Shoulder versus Look Diff. equals +5)

Example #2: My desired alignment is to hit 3 and arc 3 (a straight up shot).

Step One: Visual Target = 3 + perspective variable of (-2) = 1 = **look**

Step Two: Answer to Step One = **look** of 1 + **key** (8) = 9 = approach position straight up

Step Three: Answer to Step Two = 9 (no further computation required—straight up desired.)

Solution: Stand 9, Slide 11, Shoulder at 1, Look 1, Hit 3, Arc 3 (Shoulder versus Look Diff. equals 0)

6

Example #3: My desired alignment is to hit 5 on a 1 board point, arcing 6.

Step One: Visual Target = 5 + perspective variable of (-2) = 3 = **look**
Step Two: Answer to Step One = **look** of 3 + **key** (8) = 11 = approach
               position straight up
Step Three: Answer to Step Two = 11 - point of 1 board = 10 = final
               approach position

Solution: Stand 10, Slide 12, Shoulder at 2, Look 3, Hit 5, Arc 6 (Shoulder versus Look Diff. equals -1)

Utilization of the mathematical formulae that you have studied in this chapter will make it possible for you to compute any alignment configuration that seems to be functional (Gutter, 1st, 2nd, 3rd, 4th, or 5th Arrow, played on a straight up, swing, or point alignment). The ability to intellectually establish any method of attack will allow you to remain confident that the *arc point*, if proper physical execution is employed, will be **controlled**. The advantages that exist when you can observe the opposition's alignment, equipment, and arc, and then have the capability of duplicating that which is functional for you, from the concourse, without delivering a shot, are **immense**. Consequently, once you "get them laced up", less time will be spent in trying to figure out **where and how to play them**; thereby allowing you to focus on the task at hand in every bowling competition—**The Transition Of The Environment**. I will just bet that you thought I was going to say "throwing strikes"; if you have figured out "who, what, when, where, and why", just focus on making great shots and the score will take care of itself.

Note: This has been a very difficult chapter for me to put down into words. The premises within are much more easily taught "on the lanes". I sincerely hope that I have expressed my thoughts in an appropriate manner. If you feel you have an excellent understanding of this chapter, please continue reading; if not, read it as many times as is necessary, for it is **the foundation for all things to come!**

Chapter II:

LANE CONDITIONS
AND
MAINTENANCE PROCEDURES

The first concern of the lane maintenance personnel is "With what type of surface will I be working?" The answer to this question can be resolved if there exists an **acute awareness** of seven basic environmental aspects. They are the following:

- How long has it been since the lanes were *resurfaced*?
- How often are the lanes *recoated*?
- What is the condition of the *heads* and the *pin-decks*?
- What type of lane *finish* is being used?
- What type of lane *conditioner* (oil) is in use?
- What is the *oil pattern* (distance, width, length, and concentration)?
- What type of *cleaner* is used, and how often?

The main considerations, in setting up a playable shot, are the condition of the first 17 feet and the last 4½ feet of the lane. These are the areas that take the most abuse. The ball impacts the heads, and the pins (as well as the ball) raise havoc with the pin-deck. Since the majority of the lanes in the U.S.A. are made of wood (17 feet of maple, 42 feet of pine, and another 4½ feet of maple), with many in use for twenty-five years or more, the problem lies with maintaining a smooth, level, surface. When you are hitting the nails during resurfacing, the heads have been pumped (injecting an epoxy between the boards), the pin-decks are in a state of disrepair, and you can't seem to recoat often enough, replacement or *overlay* are the only solutions. However, either is a very expensive procedure which many proprietors cannot afford due to the current economy. Consequently, a difficult conditioning problem can manifest itself, confronting the lane man with an extremely arduous task. If a high scoring environment is desired, which seems to be the trend, you do not want hooking heads, or the ball going airborne in the pin-deck (of course, if a low scoring condition is desired, the aforementioned maladies, coupled with some *out-of-bounds* [heavy concentration of oil to the outside of the *hook spot*] are ideal). The lane man really has only one viable alternative in order to please the bowler: **high quality lane maintenance**. These are the five basic procedures that should be implemented to achieve that goal:

- Stripping the back ends every night
- Applying a liberal amount of oil in a tapered configuration
- Dragging the lanes and dusting the approaches two to three times a day
- Recoating every sixteen to eighteen weeks (dependent upon the daily lineage)
- Resurfacing every eighteen to twenty-four months (wood lanes versus "play")

Assuming that these maintenance tenets are adhered to, you will find one of the following eight conditions on the floor:

(See illustrations on page 9)

8 Basic Lane Conditions

□ Dry
▨ Lt. Oil
■ Heavy Oil

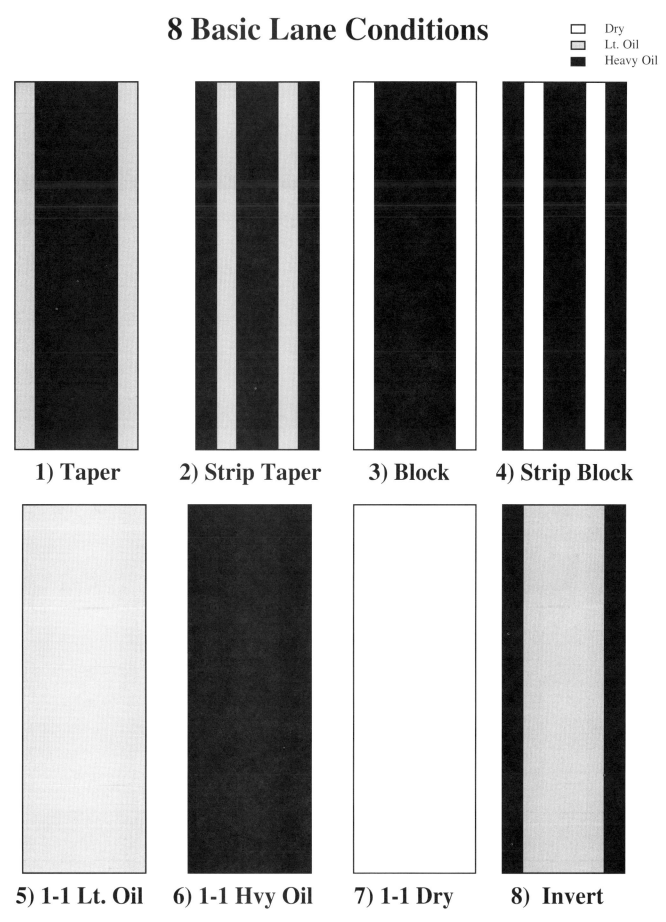

1) Taper   **2) Strip Taper**   **3) Block**   **4) Strip Block**

5) 1-1 Lt. Oil   **6) 1-1 Hvy Oil**   **7) 1-1 Dry**   **8) Invert**

* All patterns depicted are 30 feet in length.

- **The Taper**. This condition is created by providing a heavy concentration of oil to the inside, with an ever decreasing distribution to the outside, which will dramatically enhance the margin for error. You can use high compression allowance equipment (more hit) on a 2 to 5 board swing, with no fear of this high porosity equipment (texture) producing severe over and under reactions. The player will average 225-245, depending on how many games, across how many lanes.

- **The Strip Taper**. This condition is identical to the taper, except for the heavy concentration of oil to the outside. The margin for error is diminished through the creation of an out-of-bounds which can cause some problems if consistent arc-point control is not achieved. The average, for a **player**, will normally drop into the 220-235 range based upon the increased level of precision that is required.

- **The Block**. This condition has a very heavy concentration of oil on the inside of the lane with extremely dry boards to the outside. This requires the **player** to deal with severe under and over reactions. However, by using a much lower texture, on a 3 to 6 board swing, it is still a very high scoring environment. The average will be in the 215-235 range due to the low compression allowance (less hit) of the harder equipment in use.

  Note: I have seen straight players shoot 600 Over for 10 games (a 260 avg.) using High Textured Reactive Resin—Always remember, and never forget: "Horses for courses" (certain styles destroy certain conditions).

- **The Strip Block**. This condition is identical to the block, except for the heavy concentration of oil to the outside. As with the strip taper, the margin for error is diminished by the existence of the out-of-bounds, presenting the same problem of arc-point control. The average game will be in the 210-230 range based upon how close the *glaze* (out-of-bounds) is to the edge of the oil.

- **One-to-One Light Oil**. This condition is created by applying an even distribution of light oil edge to edge, thus making it much more difficult to score. The margin for error is diminished considerably because the heads hook, and the back ends get slicker due to the *carry down*. Mistakes to the inside have little or no chance of striking and the errant shots to the outside, depending on the *push* (oil build-up due to "play"), may result in a seven count, or less. Normally, the only playable zone is the *house track* (usually between 8 & 13). You must determine what equipment is functional in that area and then **make great shots**. An average game of 210 will allow you to **win** a lot of tournaments on this environment!

- **One-to-One Heavy Oil**. This condition is created by applying an even distribution of heavy oil edge to edge, thus making it very difficult to score. There are two ways to attack this pattern:

  · High texture in the house track.

  · A *fall back* (targeting inside 20, with an arc left of 17).

The margin for error is minimal when the straight player tries to play the house track (8 to 13), with 205-210 being a great game; whereas playing between the 4th and 5th arrows on a fall back will allow the power player to shoot in the 215+ range, providing they are very comfortable both visually and physically (standing 45 and looking 25, with an attempted arc of 17 to 20, for most people, looks and feels weird). However, an average of 210 will almost always make money because the difficult angle of entry (break point versus the pocket) will increase deflection adversely affecting the carry.

- **One-to-One Dry**. This condition is created by improper maintenance procedures which entail stripping the lane, and then applying no oil. You will hardly ever see this configuration because it results in terrible damage to the surface. You must use your lowest texture and play 6 to 12 boards of swing with an intended arc right of the 1st arrow. Any mistake to the inside is **history**! This allows you to miss in only one direction; therefore, an average of 210 is exceptional.

- **The Invert**. This condition can be a result of play; however, it is normally contrived to keep scores low, consisting of a heavy concentration of oil to the outside (usually boards 1 to 13, obliterating the house track) and lighter oil to the inside. This creates an **inversion** of the taper, hence its name. If your forte is playing between the 5th and 6th arrows, some remarkable results can be achieved. I actually observed a **player**, hitting 29 and arcing 16, shoot 300 on television for $50,000 on an environment that had baffled 700 people for 4 days. Normally, an average of 205-210 will get a very nice check.

Well, there you have the eight basic conditions; however, there are always variations on a theme. Changing the patterns length, width, shape (rectangle, isosceles or equilateral triangle, square, etc.), or the concentration and viscosity of the oil, with or without additives (S.T.P., Vaseline, etc.), can create a myriad of possibilities. Every player has his or her favorite shot; so, it is **imperative** that you recognize when you have the capability of emerging victorious.

REMEMBER, LUCK IS PREPARATION MEETING OPPORTUNITY!

Chapter III:

STRIKE ALIGNMENTS AND ADJUSTMENTS

In order to thoroughly take advantage of the environment, extracting all the pins possible, you must have a comprehensive understanding of how to decipher the following:

- **The correct zone**. This can be determined by two methods:

    · By watching someone who is bowling well and has a similar *speed/turn coefficient*, noting this persons hit versus arc (alignment).

    · By exploring the lane (accomplished by playing straight up 1, 5, 10, 15, and 20).

- **The correct ball**. This includes hardness, texture, and weights.

- **The method of attack**. This is straight up, a point, or a swing.

- **The mode of adjustment**. This is determined by ratio, amount, and direction.

Let us discuss these individually.

The correct zone. This is relatively easy to ascertain as long as someone, using the same arm, delivering the ball in a similar fashion, is scoring. However, if that is not the case, you must have a method of lane exploration to define the location of:

    · **The hold spot**— a concentration of oil to the inside of the lane.

    · **The hook spot**— a tapered or dry area to the outside of the hold spot.

    · **The glaze or out-of-bounds**— a build-up of oil to the outside of the hook spot.

Exploring the lane is most effective with the use of a polished, high texture, non-reactive ball. On a perfect taper (isosceles triangle or christmas tree pattern—thirty feet long with twenty units of oil at the 20th board decreasing one unit per board all the way out to the 1 board [20,19,18, etc.]) you could expect the following ball reactions:

Straight Up 1 = Brooklyn
Straight Up 5 = Nose
Straight Up 10 = Pocket
Straight Up 15 = Bucket
Straight Up 20 = Washout

A ball straight up 1 that left a washout would indicate that out-of-bounds (glaze) was present and this is simply a zone to avoid.

A ball straight up 15 (hit 15, arc 15) that missed the head pin, going away, would indicate an **extreme hook spot**. The ideal scenario is to find a place on the lane where there is **both wet inside and dry outside** that happen to be **adjacent to one another**. However, the **player** needs area in only **one direction**; allowing for the creation of area in the **opposite direction** through the utilization of the correct ball, alignment (method of attack), and mode of adjustment.

The correct ball. This, with the correct texture and weights, is such a complex issue that I will cover each aspect in its own chapter (Texture—Chapter V; Weights—Chapter VI).

The method of attack. This is relegated to the three alignments discussed in Chapter I (*straight up, swing, and point*). The **Swing** will be utilized on ninety-five percent or more of the conditions encountered. This swing is necessitated by the **under** and **over** reacting characteristics of today's high scoring environments. You should create a configuration that has the set-down point in the hold spot, with the arc point in the dry area (a minimum of 2 boards inside the glaze) so that any mistake, to the **inside** or the **outside**, has a chance of yielding a positive result. The **Straight Up** alignment will be used on the rare occasion that a **near perfect taper** is the applied maintenance procedure (less than four percent). When this unusual situation exists, it will last a very short time; then, *transition* (the constant changes brought on by heat, cold, humidity, and, most of all, play) will require you to *open up*. The **Point** is functional only when the earliest hooking ball in your arsenal will not make a move. This particular malady will occur less than one percent of the time due to the technological advances in ball manufacturing (high porosity).

The mode of adjustment. This refers to the ratio, amount, and direction. Ratio and amount may vary. Where direction is concerned, there is one simple rule: "Miss right, move right; miss left, move left". The following are the ratios to be implemented:

- **Parallel.** This refers to a 1-to-1 ratio with the feet and the target moving the same amount and the same direction. The **alignment** remains **constant**; however, the arc point (break point) moves the same amount and direction as the adjustment.

    Example: You are playing a 3 board swing 10 to 7 and decide to move 1 and 1 to the **inside**. You will still be on a 3 board *swing*, however, the ball will cross the arrows at 11 and arc at 8.

- **Zonal.** This refers to a 2 to 1 ratio, moving the feet **twice** as much as the **target**, in the same direction. The alignment will **open** or **close,** depending on the direction of the move, with the arc point remaining the same.

    Example: You are playing a 2 board swing 7 to 5 and decide to move 4 and 2 to the **outside.** You have **closed the lane** down 2 boards, with the ball now crossing the arrows at 5, maintaining the original break point (an arc of 5).

- **Abstract**. This refers to a 1 to 0 ratio, whereby you **move the feet**, with the target remaining stationary. The alignment opens or closes, with the arc point moving the same amount in the **opposite** direction of the **adjustment**.

> Example: You are playing a 4 board swing 17 to 13 and decide to move 2 and 0 to the **inside**. You have opened up the lane 2 boards and moved the arc point 2 boards to the **outside**, with the ball now crossing the arrows at 17 and arcing at 11.
> (see page 15 for illustrations)

The moves that are **normally** used are either ½, 1, 1½, or 2, depending on where the ball struck the pins (Move x Ratio = Adjustment). See Chart Below:

MOVES	PARALLEL 1 to 1	ZONAL 2 to 1	ABSTRACT 1 to 0
½ Board-High or Light Pocket	½ + ½	1 + ½	½ + 0
1 Board-Nose or Bucket	1 + 1	2 + 1	1 + 0
1½ Board-Hooking Nose or Rail	1½ + 1½	3 + 1½	1½ + 0
2 Board-Brooklyn or Washout	2 + 2	4 + 2	2 + 0

Note: The term "Hooking Nose" refers to a 3,6,10 or a 2,4,7 leave, where the ball chops the head pin off the 3 pin for the right-handed player, and the 1 pin off the 2 pin for the left-handed player. The term "Rail" refers to the 1,2,4 for the right-handed player and the 1,3,6 for the left-handed player. I assume the other terms are self-explanatory.

The proper move versus ratio is dependent upon which lane condition you are attempting to conquer. The easier the environment, the simpler the move combinations (parallel or zonal to the **inside**, with exclusive parallels to the **outside**). The tougher the environment, the more complex the move combinations (zonal or abstract to the **inside**, with parallel, zonal, or abstract, to the **outside**—juggling textures and weights when necessary). The primary concern when using similar ratios in opposite directions (zonal to the **inside**, then zonal or abstract to the **outside**), is **no counter-productive moves**. Simply stated, **do not ever move** 4 & 2 to the **inside** for a Brooklyn, and then 2 & 0, or 4 & 2, to the **outside** when the next shot leaves a washout. When confronted with this dilemma, it is normally an equipment problem (You are on a *hard wall*; which requires the use of a low textured, non-reactive ball in order to minimize the definitive *under* and *over* you are experiencing).

I consider the adjustments previously discussed in this Chapter as primary; let us discuss some secondary alternatives.

- **Reverse Abstract**. This refers to a 0 to 1 ratio, whereby the eyes move the target on the lane to the inside or the outside, in the opposite direction of the required adjustment, with the feet remaining **stationary**. The alignment opens or closes, with the arc moving in the same direction as the eyes, **twice** the original amount.

How Parallel, Zonal, and Abstract
Moves Affect the Arc and Alignment

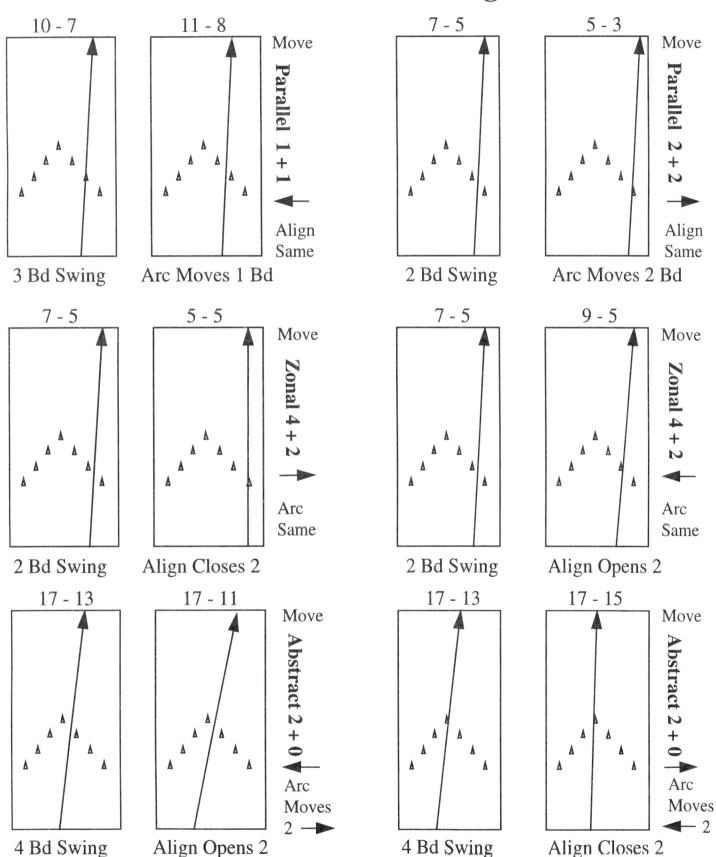

* If Left-handed
Simply transpose.

10 - 7	11 - 8		7 - 5	5 - 3
		Move		
		Parallel 1 + 1		
		Align		
		Same		
3 Bd Swing	Arc Moves 1 Bd		2 Bd Swing	Arc Moves 2 Bd

Move (right of first pair)
Parallel 1 + 1 ↑
Align
Same ←

Move (right of second pair)
Parallel 2 + 2 ↑
Align
Same →

7 - 5	5 - 5		7 - 5	9 - 5
2 Bd Swing	Align Closes 2		2 Bd Swing	Align Opens 2

Move
Zonal 4 + 2 →
Arc
Same

Move
Zonal 4 + 2 ←
Arc
Same

17 - 13	17 - 11		17 - 13	17 - 15
4 Bd Swing	Align Opens 2		4 Bd Swing	Align Closes 2

Move
Abstract 2 + 0 ←
Arc
Moves
2 →

Move
Abstract 2 + 0 →
Arc
Moves
← 2

15

Example: you are playing inside the 4th arrow, 24 to 15, and can no longer move your feet due to the ball return. The ball went Brooklyn, so you move your target to the 22 board (2 boards to the outside). This results in opening up the lane an additional 4 boards while the projected arc point becomes the 11th board.

- **Vertical moves**. This refers to visually focusing nearer or beyond your normal targeting distance. The theory behind this adjustment is that it will result in lengthening or shortening your projection, thereby creating **more skid** or **earlier hook**. I have tried to determine the appropriate distance to extend or delete per board of necessitated adjustment; unfortunately, when relegated to this method of realignment, the variables are increased due to the unusual visual images you are forcing your mind to accept. Suffice it to say, 1 foot per board of adjustment seems to be functional (dependent upon the environment). Some players also advocate moving up or back on the approach, from their normal starting position, as a method to increase or decrease ball speed. I have found six inches to twelve inches, in either direction, can make a significant difference (½ to 1 board of lateral adjustment); however, when moving forward on the approach, it is necessary to be very deliberate, or you may foul. Moving backward on the approach can result in fast feet, which may cause improper direction.

- **Hand positions**. This refers to changes made in the wrist position and/or the thumb position. Placing the wrist in a cupped position, with the thumb to the **outside**, can create additional revolutions, yielding more hook. Conversely, placing the thumb to the **inside** and breaking down the wrist will result in diminished revolutions, causing the ball to go very straight.

Coaches Corner:

I advocate delivering the ball at the same speed and rotation, utilizing every texture/weight combination, in concert with alignments and adjustments listed in this chapter, to **solve any environment**. When this has resulted in failure, the alternatives listed on this page may be your only salvation. However, you will find a few conditions to be seemingly impossible. In that case, I suggest you get the address and **never** get near that establishment again!

If you have a thorough understanding of the premises herein, read on.

Chapter IV:

SPARE ALIGNMENTS AND ADJUSTMENTS

To this point, I have dwelled on premises that allow the student to accomplish that which is paramount in the sport of ten pins: throwing strikes. In its basic context, the adage "Spare bowlers pay the entry fees, strike bowlers take home the money" may be true; however, without a second shot available, on most conditions, a 200 average would be very difficult to achieve. Spares play an integral part in the game; consequently, **you must become adept at converting** them. One of the greatest players ever to lace them up is also the best spare shooter I have ever known. I do not believe this to be coincidental. In this chapter, I intend to discuss spares, and their conversions, in great detail. We will begin with a basic formula for converting right and left-side spares off the alignments utilized for the 7 pin and the 10 pin. Two sets of differentials can be used, depending on the lane condition. They are as follows: ½, 1, 3, or 5 (normal) and 1, 2, 4, or 6 (wet or dry).

Once you have determined the proper alignment for the 7 pin, all other combinations are converted by adding the appropriate differential.

Example: You are shooting the 7 pin standing 20, looking 15; the lanes are **normal**.

Differentials	Pins	Stance	Target
½	4, 7	20 ½	15
1	4	21	15
3	2, 4, 7	23	15
5	Bucket Rail	25	15

Once you have determined the proper alignment for the 10 pin, all other combinations are converted by subtracting the appropriate differential.

Example: You are shooting the 10 pin standing 35, looking 20; the lanes are **wet**.

Differentials	Pins	Stance	Target
1	6, 10	34	20
2	6	33	20
4	3, 6, 10	31	20
6	3, 9 3, 6, 9	29	20

This system is referred to as "*Stationary off the 7 and the 10.*" I strongly recommend that when you are using this system, you should be in your lowest textured ball attempting to throw it as straight as possible.

When playing on soft conditions, some players prefer to shoot most *spare combinations off the adjusted strike alignments.* This method gives you a high percentage of conversion, as well as a read on the viability of the strike adjustment. To convert the spares that are listed, you are to make two moves before delivering the ball: first, the strike adjustment for the "leave", if you feel it is necessary, followed by; second, the spare conversion adjustment. The proper moves and most common combinations are listed below:

Leave	Strike Adjustment	Spare Adjustment
Light 8	½ & ½ Right	4 & 0 or 4 & 2 Right
Bucket	1 & 1 Right	4 & 0 or 4 & 2 Right
Rail	1½ & 1½ Right	4 & 0 or 4 & 2 Right
2,4,7	1½ & 1½ Right	6 & 0 or 6 & 3 Right
4	½ & ½ Left	8 & 0 Right or Feet 4 Right & Eyes 4 Left
4 & 7	½ & ½ Left	9 & 0 Right or Feet 5 Right & Eyes 4 Left
7	½ & ½ Left	10 & 0 Right or Feet 5 Right & Eyes 5 Left
3 or 9	3 & 1½ Left	6 & 3 Left or 3 & 0 Left
3,6,9,10	3 & 1½ Left	7 & 3 Left or 4 & 0 Left
3,6,10	3 & 1½ Left	8 & 4 Left or 5 & 1 Left

Note: The examples are for the right-handed player. If you are left-handed, simply transpose for the mirror images and move the same amount in the opposite direction (2,4,7 = 3,6,10 therefore: 3 & 1½ right—then 8 & 4 right or 5 & 1 right, etc.

Remember, this method is to be implemented **only** when the condition has a large concentration of oil in the center of the lane (*hold spot*), utilizing your strike ball and strike hand action. If your strike alignment includes a target or arc near the glaze or the gutter, use the zonal or feet and eyes adjustments; however, you may use the abstract moves as long as your target is inside 6 and you have **no** *out-of-bounds.* You are first to decide if an adjustment for the next strike ball is needed; then decide which spare adjustment is appropriate. Add the two moves together to determine your approach position and target for the spare conversion.

Some of my students are advocates of the "*Spares off the Adjusted Strike Alignment System*", and some prefer the "*Stationary off the 7 & 10 System*". Use the one that is most functional for **you**. Now, let us discuss the remaining spare combinations and the proper adjustments.

Leave	Strike Adjustment	Spare Adjustment
5 or 5,8	½ & ½ Right	Use New Strike Alignment
5 & 9	4 & 2 Left	2 & 1 or 1 & 0 Left
1,2,4 & 10	2 & 2 Right	5 & 2 or 5 & 0 Right
5-7 Split	½ & ½ Right	5 & 2 or 4 & 0 Left
6,7,10 Split	2 & 1 Left	1½ Left of 10 Pin Align.
4,7,10 Split	2 & 1 Left	1½ Right of 7 Pin Align.
1,3,6,10	Seriously consider changing Ball, Alignment, Arc, and Zone!	

Note: Once again, the examples are for the right-handed player; if you are left-handed, simply transpose and move the same amount in the opposite direction (the 1,2,4 & 10 for the right-handed player = 1,3,6 & 7 for the left-hander; therefore, the appropriate combination of moves would be: 2 & 2 left—then 5 & 2 or 5 & 0 left, etc.).

One very important factor when discussing the appropriate methods for shooting spares is the **proper angular mode of the upper body**, based upon the spare in question. This can be achieved by positioning your feet on the approach, then rotating your hips and aligning your bowling shoulder on a perpendicular (ninety degrees) with the point at which you would like your ball to strike the pin or pins in question (some bowlers prefer to angle their **feet** as well). This visual imaging simplifies the execution. Remember, a bowling ball has a diameter of approximately 8¾ inches and the pins are approximately 4¾ inches wide; therefore, you have approximately a 13½ inch margin for error on a 7 pin or a 10 pin, and 22¼ inches on all other one pin spares. Consequently, the only excuse for missing spares, other than terrible execution, is **improper alignment**.

Coaches Corner:
Please make sure that you take great care when establishing your *system of choice*, *equipment*, *hand action*, and/or *angular mode*. Believe me, you really begin to appreciate the **spare game** when, after bowling a Monday Morning Qualifier ("rabbit squad") on the P.B.A. Tour, you observed that a score of 120 under, for ten games (188 average), had received an entry into the Tournament. If all your emphasis has been on the strike ball, **think again**; **spares count, too!**

Chapter V:

TEXTURES

When discussing textures, there are seven basic categories:

- Hard Rubber (82-92 hardness on the durometer)
- Soft Rubber (75-81)
- Hard Plastic (82-92)
- Soft Plastic (75-81)
- Hard Urethane (82-92)
- Soft Urethane (75-81)
- Reactive Resin (75-85)

The texture or porosity (friction capabilities) of a bowling ball affects the reaction much more than interior density. The major differential, in the coefficient of friction of today's equipment, is the physical properties utilized in the construction of each ball. In the 60's, not a lot was known about surface preparation (sanding, polishing, finessing, etc.); therefore, most bowlers simply put three holes in the ball and went about the business of "knocking down the wood". Due to the high friction qualities of the lacquer finishes, the hard rubber and hard plastic balls, which were available at the time, worked very nicely. However, the early 70's brought about changes in lane finishes (urethane replaced lacquer) and maintenance procedures (higher viscosity oils and vastly improved lane machines); consequently, the professional was confronted with an extremely unique problem: "How do I hook the ball?" One answer was to "soak" a plastic ball (they were immersed in solutions like M.E.K. or Toulene) thereby changing its molecular structure. This dramatically affected the surface texture as the ball would literally "hook on ice". I truly believe that when the "soaker" was outlawed, the equipment revolution was put into high gear. The subsequent introductions of "The Bleeder", "The Urethane Ball", and "The Reactive Resin Ball" changed the face of the game forever!

The manufacturers of bowling balls are merely filling a need; however, in solving one problem, they create another: **"Which ball do I use today?"** Many of the bowlers make the same mistake. They try to use reactive resin equipment on every environment due to the high compression allowance (ability of the ball to recover its shape upon impact) and the high coefficient of restitution (a ball's capability to maintain original momentum after impact) yielding tremendous hit. This is partially due to the misconception that a hard, low friction, non-reactive ball will not hit; which is not always the case. The primary concern when attempting to create power at impact is *skid/hook ratio*; therefore, compression allowance is secondary. If you are using the correct piece of equipment, the ball will precess continuously and, at the intended arc point (due to increased friction caused by a tilted axis becoming more vertical), begin hooking toward the pocket. If you are able to achieve this reaction, and the back ends have not become too slick, a "brick" will knock down ten pins.

It is very important that you realize what texture is appropriate for the lane condition on which you are competing. Therefore, you must have some "frames of reference."

- **Too High**: An indication that you are using a texture that is **too high** would be a ball hooking prior to the intended arc point and then "rolling out," resulting in too much deflection (no skid-no hook: no hook-no hit). A ball that hooks instantly, missing the head pin going away, would also indicate a need to switch to a lower texture.

- **Too Low**: An indication that the texture is **too low** would be a delayed break point, resulting in abnormal deflection due to inappropriate axis tilt. A ball that skids 63 feet through the pin deck would definitely suggest the use of a higher texture.

Coaches Corner:

- If the heads are **oily** and the area to the outside, along with the **back end** is **dry**, non-reactive urethane or plastic will be very functional.

- If the heads are **hooking**, and the area **outside** as well as the **back end** is **oily**, reactive resin may be your only **viable** alternative.

The science of "*Shell Preparation*," to alter the surface friction content, thereby changing the skid-hook ratio, has become required knowledge for the professional. One method, that allows the use of the *highest compression allowance equipment* possible, is referred to as "*Finessing and Polishing*." The ball is sanded with 180 grit (very coarse) gradually increasing to 1500 grit (very fine) and then polish is applied. This process creates an ultra-smooth surface, reducing potential friction, which enhances the "Reservation of Power." Regardless of the surface preparation you choose, constant monitoring is paramount. Whether the ball is normal, polished, finessed and polished, or sanded, it should be returned to its desired state after use (five games or more). Implementing this principle will allow you, when noting *lane transition* (push, heads hooking, carry-down, etc.), to make every ball change with a great degree of confidence.

I think it is important for the reader to understand that, before the advent of reactive resin technology, the "tweeners" (intermediate rotation) were **history** when the heads hooked and the back ends were oily. They were forced to use a lower texture, lower compression allowance ball to get through the front end of the lane, resulting in inadequate "**hit**" on the back end (no carry-no cash). Fortunately, science has created a "more level playing field." However, **be advised, there is no substitute for hand action**. A powerful hand release on today's lane finishes and oiling patterns **usually** results in more **margin for error** and **better carry**. If you throw the ball straighter than the average player, your only alternative is **excellent tactics**. Understanding textures and texture preparation is just one more step in the developmental process.

I believe that **life is** not about knowing all the answers, but merely **understanding the questions**. I hope this chapter has succeeded in that area of expertise. Once you have a comprehension of **textures**, you can further enhance your abilities as a **player** by becoming knowledgeable on the complex subject of **weights**. Please, continue.

Chapter VI:

WEIGHTS

Weights: a seven-letter word with infinite variations. I will endeavor to simplify this complex subject without diminishing its importance. When referring to the sphere that we use, commonly known as a "bowling ball", there are seven separate areas of concern when determining the dynamic (ball in motion) and static imbalances. They are the following:

- Top Weight
- Bottom Weight
- Finger Weight
- Thumb Weight
- Positive-Side Weight
- Negative-Side Weight
- Gross Weight

Top versus bottom. You are allowed a three ounce differential when weighing the top and the bottom of the ball. Top weight increases the skid on the front-end—reserving hook for the back end. Bottom weight does just the opposite—producing early hook thereby diminishing the back-end reaction. The amount of top weight that a ball has, prior to drilling, and the position it is placed, dictates the potential for change in the skid/hook ratio. Once you have determined your normal displacement (the amount of weight removed when drilling the finger holes and the thumb hole) you can decide on the top weight necessary based on what imbalances you desire.

Finger versus thumb. You are allowed a one ounce differential between the two. Finger weight increases the skid, reserving power (hook) for the back end. Thumb weight causes the ball to precess faster (hook earlier) thereby diminishing the back-end reaction.

Positive versus Negative Side. You are allowed a one ounce differential from side to side. Positive side increases the skid slightly, but affects the back-end reaction much more dramatically—enhancing the hook. Negative side decreases the skid pattern; which, in turn, diminishes the flip (back end reaction).

Gross Weight. You are allowed to use a ball that weighs as much as sixteen pounds; but not one sixty-fourth of an ounce more. The heavier the ball, the less deflection you can expect; however, some of the high revolution players have gone to equipment as light as fifteen pounds. This is to decrease the power at impact due to the reservation of power and compression allowance factors in the reactive resin equipment.

In summary, top, finger, and positive-side weights **induce skid**, reserving the power for the back end. Bottom, thumb, and negative-side weights diminish the skid, causing the ball to **hook earlier** which decreases the back-end reaction.

Through analysis of the previous chapter and the first page in this chapter, you now have a basic concept of textures and weights, and how each, independently, can affect the skid/hook ratio of a bowling ball. I will now discuss some particulars by creating a variety of environments and attempting to solve the problems each condition presents with the two aspects working in unison.

- **Hooking Heads — Tight Back Ends.** This condition requires skid weights up front and hook weights for the back end. Any time you are confronted with this environment, immediately reach for a polished, reactive resin ball in a leverage state. The top weight should be one ounce or more. The positive side should be rendered to one-half to three-fourths ounce and you should have one-half to three-fourths ounce finger weight. This combination of texture and weights creates above average skid with maximum flip (hook). The tactically sound power player would like to bowl on this all the time!

- **Tight Heads — Hooking Back Ends.** This condition requires a weight distribution that will not leave the player with the dreaded over and under reaction. I recommend label weight, pin in. The texture of choice, until *carry-down* occurs, is a soft, polished, non-reactive, urethane ball. The distribution I find to be very functional is zero to one-half ounce top, zero to one-fourth finger, and one-fourth negative side (achieved with a balance hole [void]). Everybody that can *play* will shoot "telephone numbers".

  Note: The average speed, high-revolution player may have to use a lower texture with similar weights. The straighter player can use more top and positive side.

- **Hooking Heads — Hooking Back Ends.** This condition requires weights that will get the ball down the lane but not give too violent of a reaction on the back end. I recommend label weight, pin in. The texture must be your lowest available; preferably hard rubber or hard plastic. The distribution should be low top (zero to one-half ounce) with three-fourths to seven-eighths finger and one-half to three-fourths negative side (voided). The low texture, with the finger weight, will create the necessary skid with the other characteristics yielding the proper back-end reaction. The straight players will think they have found heaven.

- **Tight Heads — Tight Back Ends.** This condition requires weights that will allow the ball to hook at the proper break point and still hit. It really depends on **how** the player delivers the ball when choosing the right texture/weight combination. The high speed, high revolution competitor can use half axis or axis in a sanded, reactive or a sanded, soft urethane. The average speed, average revolution player can use axis leverage or leverage placed into a sanded, reactive resin or a sanded, soft urethane. The proper set-up for each person is totally dictated by which combination yields the largest *margin for error* coupled with the *best carry*.

These four conditions depict **ninety percent** of the environments you will encounter in your travels on the tournament highway. In order to be totally prepared for any eventuality, you must understand the different ball drilling combinations available to the player; and, more importantly, how they are supposed to be arrived at by the person you entrust to drill your equipment. Let us discuss the **seven** most commonly used by the professionals.

I will list them, and then address each one individually. (See page 25 for illustrations).

- Label
- Half Leverage
- Leverage
- Half Axis
- Axis
- Leverage Axis
- Flip Leverage

Label. This requires the center of mass and the center of gravity (pin-in) to be positioned six and three-fourths inches from the axis. The anticipated reaction is one of maximum skid with average hook.

Half Leverage. This is also a pin-in configuration, located five and one-sixteenth inches from the axis. The skid pattern is diminished, resulting in an increased hook on the back end.

Leverage. The pin is located three and three-eights inches from the player's axis. There has been some discussion as to pin-in versus pin-out when drilling this particular distribution. I believe the proper set-up is left to the individual's judgement. The expected reaction is one of average skid followed by maximum flip (hook) due to the tremendous reservation of power promoted by this configuration.

Half Axis. The center of mass is placed one and eleven-sixteenths inches from the axis. This lay-out produces a diminished skid pattern, which results in less back-end reaction.

Axis. You must have a ball, pin-in, with very low top weight, for the best results. The pin is placed directly on your axis. This set-up will result in very early hook with the ball going extremely straight on the back end.

Leverage Axis. This is one of the weight distributions referred to by some as *exotic*. It is established by placing the *center of gravity* (C.G.) in the axis position with the *center of mass* (C.M.) in the leverage position. The expected ball reaction is somewhat of a combination of leverage and axis, hence its name. The ball will precess slightly slower than an axis-weighted piece of equipment, but it will still hook hard on the back end. *"Trick ball"* might aptly describe this unique drilling. To accomplish this unorthodox layout, you should try to find a ball with a pin-out exactly three and three-eights inches for best results in reference to what is expected.

Flip Leverage. Another of the exotic variety, this distribution requires the C.G. and the C.M. to be placed three and three-eighths inches from the axis. In order to accomplish this, you need a ball with the pin-out approximately one and a half to two inches; then, the label is twisted ninety degrees. The pin is now up by the fingers, leaving the center of gravity in the leverage position. If you draw three lines, one from the axis to the pin, then from the pin to the C.G., and then from the C.G. to the axis, you will observe an isosceles triangle laying on its side. The expected ball reaction is similar to pin-in leverage.

Diagram of 7 Basic Weights

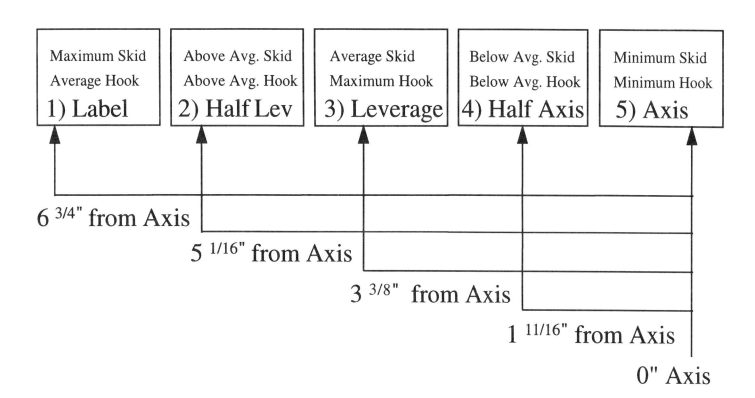

Maximum Skid Average Hook 1) Label	Above Avg. Skid Above Avg. Hook 2) Half Lev	Average Skid Maximum Hook 3) Leverage	Below Avg. Skid Below Avg. Hook 4) Half Axis	Minimum Skid Minimum Hook 5) Axis

6 3/4" from Axis

5 1/16" from Axis

3 3/8" from Axis

1 11/16" from Axis

0" Axis

*** Void, Size, and Position
based on top weight Requirements**

CM = Center of Mass
CG = Center of Gravity

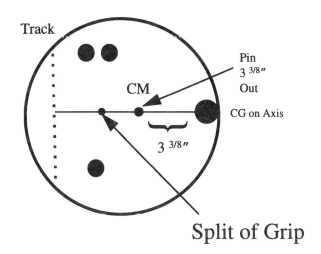

Leverage Axis

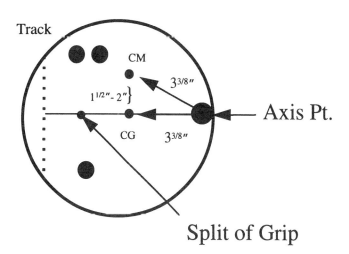

Flip Leverage

When deciding on which of the seven configurations you desire, please be very careful where top weight and the position of the balance hole (void), is concerned. I recommend high top (three and one-half ounces or more) if drilling a leverage or flip leverage configuration. I prefer low top (two ounces or less) in the axis and half axis configurations. If you are drilling a label configuration, depending, as always, on the player's speed/turn coefficient, I would normally use two and one-half to three ounces top weight. The balance hole presents the competitor with several alternatives. Personally, I like six and three-fourths inches perpendicular to the center line at the split of the grip. This method removes side weight without disturbing the top to bottom, or finger to thumb, distribution. The seven and one-half to nine inch void is also a popular choice, as it removes the necessary side weight and adds top weight. Be aware that a balance hole on the axis does not create a dynamic (a ball in motion) imbalance, only a static (a ball at rest) imbalance; if you drill the void anywhere else, it will affect the skid/hook ratio.

Coaches Corner:

Once you find someone you trust to prepare your equipment, listen to any and all suggestions. Above all, where weights and textures are concerned, experiment. Remember, what works for someone else, may not work for you; conversely, you may win a national title with a combination no one else can use.

Chapter VII:

THE ARSENAL

Once you have achieved a full comprehension of *lane conditions, textures,* and *weights*, you are in the enviable position of having the necessary expertise to design your own personal *arsenal*. After all, we are at war with the environment. To win any battle you must understand the enemies strengths and weaknesses. The lane has one major advantage over its opponents: *constant transition* (heads dry out; back ends become slick; oil is pushed to the outside diminishing the swing area). However, the lane has two major weaknesses that can certainly be exploited by the tactically sound player: it cannot avoid being attacked by moving out of the way; and, the pins cannot jump over the bowling ball. Once you have determined the proper arc point, the correct alignment, and the applicable mode of adjustment, the only decision remaining is that of the proper ball. Since there are hundreds of singular products available, you must simplify when creating a selection that seemingly covers every contingency. I will relate to you an arsenal of twelve balls with various exterior and interior design components, weights, and surface preparations; one of which will allow you to "get to the pocket and carry" on any lanes that have been dressed with a playable maintenance procedure.

1. High texture, non-reactive, 2 piece, axis-leverage, heavily sanded.

2. High texture, non-reactive, 2 piece, label, polished.

3. Low texture, non-reactive, 2 piece, label, rendered negative, polished.

4. Hard plastic, 3 piece, label, rendered negative, finessed & polished.

5. High texture, reactive resin, 2 piece, axis leverage, sanded (400 grit).

6. High texture, reactive resin, 2 piece, half leverage, polished.

7. Intermediate texture, reactive resin, 2 piece, half leverage, polished.

8. Low texture, reactive resin, 3 piece, half leverage, finessed and polished.

9. High texture, reactive resin, 3 piece, leverage, sanded (400 grit).

10. High texture, reactive resin, 3 piece, leverage, polished.

11. Intermediate texture, reactive resin, 3 piece, Leverage, finessed and polished.

12. High texture, reactive resin, 3 piece, flip leverage, polished.

When considering each piece of equipment, your speed/turn coefficient will dictate the amount of top weight used and the exact surface preparation (the high speed, high revolution player may want to use "finger-negative" or "thumb-negative" in balls 6, 7 and 8 to eliminate the over and under the "positive pin placement" could create). Some of you may find a need for additional bowling balls and still some others may be saying "Why so many?" These are merely suggestions based upon what I have found to work for the majority of my students on a wide variety of conditions. The more time and money you have, the more you can experiment. However, I strongly suggest that if and when the size of your arsenal begins to cause more problems than it is solving, pare it down.[2]

Obviously, I have mentioned no brand names. I believe that each individual player must decide what products are best for his or her game. In my travels, one of the most commonly heard commentaries is: "I know it worked for you; but, I can't get that ball to react properly for me, regardless of the weight distribution or texture preparation." Always remember, and do not ever forget: **horses for courses**! Once you have found a few companies whose products work for you, stick with them by setting up a variety of weight, texture, and surface preparation combinations. Remember, there are no *magic balls*—only *magic people*! Work very hard on becoming a *player* through developing a solid physical and tactical foundation. Once that is accomplished, you can then address the mysteries of textures and weights which were discussed in the previous two chapters. If the entire puzzle is properly pieced together, you will, most certainly, be a force to reckon with.

The next chapter will address the problem of increasing your level of expertise through *proper practice procedures*. Utilizing this time correctly can enable you to realize your full potential. Please, continue.

---

[2]If you wish to possess a quality ball transporter (a three-wheel dolly capable of carrying four double-ball bags (8 balls) with ease) please call:408-374-3340 or write to M & W Products, 985 Hacienda, Campbell, CA 95008.

Chapter VIII:

PRACTICE PROCEDURES

There is an old saying that goes "Practice makes perfect." Perfection is seldom, if ever, achieved in the sport of bowling; however, with *perfect practice procedures*, your chances of realizing the ultimate goal of every bowler, which is to shoot a 300, are definitely enhanced. This quest for perfection causes most bowlers to attempt to strike on every shot during a practice session. In my opinion, *proper practice* should entail four basic facets:

- Development of a solid physical game (control of speed, direction, drift pattern, and rotation)

- Achieving visual and physical comfort from a variety of zones (2 board to 22 board) and alignments (2 board point to a 6 board swing)

- Learning equipment differentials (comparing various weight and texture combinations)

- Development of a solid spare game (conversions off the strike alignments versus conversions off a stationary target)

Let us discuss each of these facets individually.

Development of a solid physical game. Where the physical game is concerned, you must have total control of four specific aspects:

- **Speed**. Appropriate ball speed is in direct correlation to a person's hand action; the higher the amount of revolutions imparted to the ball, the faster it must be delivered. Approach length, the number of steps, and the height of the push-away are factors that can dramatically change your pace, which will raise or lower your ball speed.

- **Direction**. The ability to hit a target consistently is predicated upon one specific factor: **focus**. Assuming that you have acceptable timing, maintaining visual contact with your target, until the ball has passed through it, is paramount. Simple rule: **do not peek**! Forget about the destination and enjoy the journey. Place all of your focus on execution— not the results. If you strike, hurray; if you do not put "ten in the pit" and have made a good shot, adjust!

- **Drift pattern**. Only through concentrated effort can you become aware of what your drift is regarding direction and amount. If you think "walk straight," regardless of the alignment, most good athletes will standardize their pattern, dependent upon the area of the lane they are playing. Once the drift is understood, you are assured of arc-point control; which, in my opinion, is "the essence of the game".

- **Rotation**. This is commonly referred to as *hand action*. It can be improved through a conscious thought process of simultaneously lifting up the back and turning around the side of the ball. Pitches, grips, and wrist supports can all be used to aid in the process of creating a powerful hand release; more revs equals more area and better hit. However, understand that each person will realize his or her limitations in this area of expertise. Simple rule: stay within yourself!

Achieving visual and physical comfort from a variety of alignments and zones. The idea behind this concept is for you to be able to control your own destiny, regardless of when, where, how, or why the current environment exists. The premise is simplistic in nature, but very complex in application. The player is required to create a variety of possible alignments (set down, target, arc) so as to experience the visual imagery and physical sensations that occur across the lane. You are attempting to become equally adept at playing 2 straight up versus 22 on a 6 board swing. Every person has their favorite shot; however, if you practice properly you will be prepared to deal with the unique, or the unusual, in a league or tournament atmosphere.

Learning equipment differentials. This particular dilemma must be resolved satisfactorily due to the number of balls that are carried by the average professional (nine to twelve); with most amateurs using three to six pieces of equipment. Redundancy in an arsenal is unbecoming; therefore, it is imperative to set it up in such a fashion that each ball does something different (earlier or later hook; more or less flip). Drilling techniques and texture preparations are only half the battle; you must know how each ball reacts on a similar environment. This can be achieved by lining up with a specific ball and then determining the differentials between it and the rest of your arsenal. Certain conditions will indicate minute moves (1 & ½ or 2 & 1) in order to realign when changing equipment; however, other conditions will require major adjustments (4 & 2 or 6 & 3) when comparing the same equipment. Do your initial testing on somewhat of a normal set-up; not one-to-one dry or one-to-one wet. Remember: if the ball in question is designed to go long and flip hard, you can expect it to go sixty-three feet on a wet lane; conversely, if the ball you are using is designed to hook early and the lanes are dry, do not be dismayed if it rolls out at forty-five feet.

Developing a solid spare game. It doesn't matter how well you are lined up and executing. You are not going to strike every time. When you leave a pin or pins, you must convert or be faced with "throwing a three-bagger" or "doubling twice" just to score 200+. Making your spares takes a tremendous amount of pressure off the delivery of the next strike ball. If you are not confident of certain spare combinations (bucket, rail, washout, 2-4-7, 3-6-10 etc.), you should attempt a variety of texture, hand position, target, and approach position variations until you find something that looks and/or feels comfortable as well as being functional. In a previous chapter, I discussed the two most common methods of spare conversion techniques (stationary and off the adjusted strike alignment). Many professionals prefer the *stationary method* using a hard plastic ball delivered with a flat hand release and high speed regardless of the environment. I teach the utilization of *adjustments off the strike alignments* **if there is hold** (concentration of oil in the center of the lane). My suggestion is that you use both systems, when hold exists, and determine which provides you with the highest percentage of conversions and stick with that method. **When there is no hold**, you must use the *stationary system* for best results; taking the condition "out of play" is paramount.

If, after reading this chapter, you have any questions about proper practice procedures, please read Chapter VIII one more time. If you don't have any questions, we will now discuss physical conditioning; a facet of bowling that is often overlooked, even by some of the professionals.

Chapter IX:

PHYSICAL CONDITIONING

Remaining in good physical condition is very important for any professional athlete regardless of the sport. Strength and stamina spell longevity. To produce these two qualities, you must adhere to a strict regimen. The following formula has enabled many sports personalities to remain competitive long past their prime. You have four areas you must relate to:

- **Diet and Vitamin Supplements**

- **Cardio-Vascular Training**

- **Weight Training**

- **The Hand and The Wrist**

Let us talk about each, individually.

Diet and vitamin supplements. Proper eating habits and vitamin supplements can produce a very healthy body; which includes high protein (meat, fish, chicken etc.) and low carbohydrates, eliminating fats and starches, and staying away from any foods with high sugar content (ice cream, cakes, soda pop, etc.). Any recognized daily vitamin supplement is sufficient; however, one of the finest players I have ever known took vitamins recommended by a nutritionist and swore that this was one of the main reasons for his longevity. Suffice it to say, a healthy body promotes a healthy mind; therefore, any program that is functional for you is acceptable.

Cardio-vascular training. "A strong heart yields a strong body" may be the cliche of the 90's; however, exercising this organ certainly cannot hurt. I have found several very good programs for this purpose:

- **Stationary Bicycle** (15-20 minutes)

- **Stair-Master** (15-20 minutes)

- **Walking** (1-2 miles per day)

The last two also aid in the conditioning of the lower body (legs) which plays a very important role in achieving proper leverage, facilitating proper projection and extension. Remember, whatever regimen you choose, be consistent.

Weight training. I feel that leg and upper body strength are the two most important areas. It is not necessary to use free weights (dumb-bells, bar-bells, etc.); any good fitness center has equipment that is based on weight resistance. Keep the resistance minimal and the repetitions high. The following devices are the ones that I have found to be most functional:

- **Bench Press**
- **"Lat" or Butterfly Press**
- **Leg Press**
- **Hip Press**
- **Bicep Curls**

These five devices properly isolate the areas that suffer the most fatigue when bowling. I recommend two sets of 15-25 repetitions on each device three times a week when possible. If you are a regular touring player, your frequency will most assuredly be less; however, I have heard the term "work-out freaks" used to describe two of the most successful players over the past ten years. Obviously, physical fitness has a definite up-side.

The hand and the wrist. Regardless of the sport, the hand and the wrist play very important roles. Whether hitting a tennis or golf ball, throwing a baseball, or shooting a basketball, you must be able to rely on these two parts of the body to do their job. However, throwing a 15-16 pound bowling ball, at eighteen miles an hour, with eighteen revolutions, most certainly is not what the wrist and the hand were originally designed for; therefore, great care must be taken where strengthening and preventative maintenance are concerned. Let us discuss each task individually.

- **Strengthening**. Two devices work for this purpose:

  - Excel Hand Exerciser (isolates the hand: fingers and thumb)

  - Marcy's Wedge (isolates tendons and ligaments in the wrist)

Both of these products are available at any good athletic supply store. However, if you cannot afford the investment, a tennis ball and a ten pound piece of iron will suffice.

- **Preventative Maintenance**. Two methods work for this purpose:

  - Wrapping the wrist with self-adhesive gauze and/or adhesive tape.

  - Applying ice, mentholatum, and a heating pad after bowling.

Bowling, on a physical level, yields very gradual attrition. However, to remain successful over the long haul, your body must be able to do what the mind requests; therefore, there is no substitute for physical fitness. I hope you find that eating correctly, ingesting vitamins, and exercising properly increases both your strength and your stamina. If you have a thorough understanding of this chapter, please read on!

Chapter X:

MENTAL CONDITIONING

A few million individuals are gifted with remarkable athleticism (hand-eye coordination and exceptional musculature). Only a small percentage of these ever become professional athletes. I feel there are four basic reasons for this phenomenon, comprised by the presence, or the lack, of the following items:

- **Desire**
- **Ambition**
- **Hard Work**
- **Mental Conditioning**

The first three are foregone conclusions to a successful career in any field of endeavor; the fourth reason for success or failure is neither quite so obvious nor so easy to cultivate. Mental Conditioning is developing the capability, in a stress-filled situation, to interact or react in a calm, cool, collected manner. You must be able to recognize your adversary and deal with this animate or inanimate object in an intelligent, objective fashion.

In order for the brain to function properly, regardless of the dilemma with which it is confronted, we must have some concept of how it operates; because once the physical requirements are filled, **the use of the mind separates the winners from the losers**. It has been said that sport is one hundred percent mental. You may disagree with this premise, but please understand that body parts can only be mobilized through neuron transfer; the mind requests movement, at which point the brain sends electrical impulses that cause the muscles to contract which promotes motion. Therefore, if the brain does not send any impulses, there isn't any movement; which would make delivering a bowling ball virtually impossible. Consequently, **bowling is one hundred percent mental**. Hey, don't yell at me, it's only a theoretical concept; however, I believe that it does warrant some serious consideration. Understanding the basic structure of the brain should allow the individual to control some of the variables wherein thoughts produce physical responses.

The brain is composed of the **conscious mind** (twelve percent) and the **subconscious mind** (eighty-eight percent). The **conscious mind** is responsible for thought; it has the capacity for deductive reasoning and idea formulation through assimilation and application of information. The **subconscious mind** will facilitate appropriate physical responses, regardless of the conscious pressures, but only through intense training. This consists of developing "condition reflexes" or "muscle memory" (a misnomer, for muscles have no memory); which is accomplished through repetition of the same action (lift, turn, pace, drift, etc.). The theory is that if you repeat a physical act enough times, the subconscious will be able to intervene when you are consciously distraught (too nervous, scared, or distracted to achieve the proper results). For all intents and purposes, your subconscious mind can be used as a *fail-safe mechanism*.

One of the most important aspects of functioning in a stress-filled environment is the *pre-shot routine*. This is achieved in bowling by implementing a sequential thought process, prior to every delivery, from which the player never deviates; regardless of the success or failure of the previous shot. I have found the following sequence to be very functional:

PRE-SHOT ROUTINE

1. Determine your target
2. Determine your approach position
3. Choose the ball you intend to use
4. Step up on the approach and position your feet
5. Place your hand in the ball
6. Focus on your target
7. Remind yourself to walk straight
8. Begin your approach; maintaining visual contact with, and reaching through, your target
9. Note the ball reaction—if an adjustment is required, compute the proper ratio and amount, recording the new stance, target, and arc, in your mind.

Once you have bowled twenty-five to fifty games, you will find the conscious check list has shrunken to four, or less, items (example: focus, walk straight, reach). I have found this process to be very helpful in pressure situations. The intensified thought allows the player to focus on the execution, rather than the outcome, while maintaining a relaxed demeanor. Simply stated, you are so busy thinking, you do not have time to **choke**; which is nothing more than **allowing your emotions to overcome your powers of reason**! I believe this response is predicated upon a lack of understanding regarding the normal reactions of human beings when cast into stressful circumstances. The following are to be expected in said situations:

- **Clammy Hands**

- **A Queasy Stomach**

- **Shaky Knees**

- **Blurred Vision**

- **Accelerated Heart Beat**

If, and when, you learn to relate to these reactions as being normal, you have conquered a very formidable enemy. These five factors can never be totally controlled; however, the harder you concentrate on the task at hand, the less you are aware of the negatives and the easier it becomes to accentuate the positives. Remember, the lane cannot move and the pins will not jump over your ball. If the alignment, weights, texture, and arc point are correct, a well-executed shot will result in a strike. Your adversaries, in the sport of bowling, are inanimate objects; consequently, they have no control over the outcome of a given delivery. In this sport, you are indeed the "*master of your own destiny*." I teach all of my students to enjoy the journey, and do not be concerned about the destination.

35

Thinking "score" will produce improper execution; this sport is "*played from the neck up.*" The grammar may be incorrect, but the point I am trying to make is no less valid; focus on proper execution and the score will take care of itself!

In a society where Winners are idolized and Losers are demeaned, it is very important to understand what the qualifications are for each status. While I was studying the martial arts, competition against a superior foe was required in order to achieve "*belt promotions*". I learned, through defeat, that emerging victorious was not the primary goal. My "*sensei*" believed, as I do now, that performing to your full mental and physical capabilities (giving one hundred percent) is the only determining factor when considering who won and who lost. A winner gives all he or she has; a loser gives something less. Where you "*finish*" is irrelevant; how "*well you perform*" is the primary concern.

That experience taught me a very valuable lesson: **you must embrace failure** in order to progress. Victory makes you aware that the potential for success exists; only through analysis of your defeats can you find the potential for improvement. Some people I have met believe that "*analysis is paralysis*". My comment to them is "*If you don't learn to analyze, one day you will end up paralyzed.*" Human beings are prone to repeat the same mistakes throughout their lives; therefore, you must remember that "*failure is your friend,*" for it is your best teacher. Confront the problem, find a solution to the dilemma, and then, move on.

If your aspirations include joining the P.B.A. or the L.P.B.T., be aware that the main difference on a professional level is that the majority of the players have figured out a way to minimize their errors; they may not always **win** a match, but they seldom **lose** one. It is my belief that the key to success lies within the **preparation**. Do you want to be a winner? Then spend some time studying the work ethics of those who have already achieved that exalted position, and you will find two constants: "*Luck is the residue of hard work!*" and "*If you fail to plan, you plan to fail.*" I hope that this chapter has given you a "*method to your madness.*" Well, that should be **enough cliches** for one day.

The next two chapters should provide additional insight into proper preparation and maintenance. If you have a firm grasp of the tenets expressed in this chapter, please, feel free to continue!

Chapter XI:

TOOLS OF THE TRADE

I feel, in order to be competitive on all levels, you must carry a few basic necessities other than bowling balls to enable you to achieve your highest potential regardless of the problems that might occur. I believe that these are the products required:

- An Accessory Bag that contains:

    · Adhesive Tape — pre-cut ¾" and/or 1" wide
    · Plastic Tape ¾" wide (red and green)
    · Scissors and/or a Pocket-knife
    · Rosin Bag
    · Sandpaper (180 grit)
    · Shoelaces (two pair)
    · Easy Slide and/or Scotch-brite Pads
    · Wire Shoebrush
    · Fingernail Clippers
    · Emery Board (for sanding calluses)
    · Lighter Fluid or Alcohol (cleaning)
    · Nu-Skin or Cut-Patch
    · Bevel Knife
    · Thumb Savers (teflon inserts)

- Three or Four Clean Towels

- Two Pairs of Bowling Shoes (slick or tacky approaches)

- My Manual (in case you might want a refresher course)

In addition to the items previously listed, I feel that some players may need a better fit, better feel, more support, and/or revolution enhancement. There are several devices available—each filling a specific need. I do not necessarily recommend them; however, if any are functional for you, make an effort to have them available. The products listed have solved a wide variety of problems for several of my students—both amateur and professional. I will attempt to give an indication as to the designated function of each item:

- Cobra — enhances lateral rotation
- Scorpion — enhances lift
- Robbies Wrister — prevents breaking of the wrist
- Don Carter Glove — promotes an earlier thumb release
- Weber Wristmaster — firms the wrist
- Scalia Splint — absorbs arm strain
- Mongoose — enhances lift and turn
- Pro-Release — enhances lift and turn
- Perfect-Wrister — enhances rotation

- Thumb Inserts — provide a better fit and/or feel
- Finger Grips — increases revolutions; better fit and/or feel
- Bowling Gloves — better feel; enhances rotation

Obviously I have not included every device that is available. I believe that any product which produces positive results for you should become one of your **tools**. If you feel enhancement is needed is a certain area, but you are not sure of what to purchase, consult with one of the local pro shops, or a P.B.A. Member, and ask for their opinion. The primary concern is to be informed about any new innovations in equipment and/or accessories. I suggest that you subscribe to the "Bowlers Journal" because it is a well-written monthly publication that will keep you abreast of current trends in the sport.

The purpose of this chapter is to enable you to arrive, at any and all bowling events, totally prepared. If your "tool chest" is properly outfitted you will never be distracted from the task at hand because you had to ask a fellow competitor for something that you forgot. I always made it a habit to carry two of everything whenever possible; if something was lost or stolen, I always had a spare. Now that we have covered the *tools of the trade* let us discuss some of the *tricks of the trade*.

Chapter XII:

TRICKS OF THE TRADE

The title of this chapter essentially speaks for itself. It refers to that which is seldom, if ever, discussed in public by the top players. In the interest of fair play, I would like to bring a few tricks to your attention.

- **Taping a ball**. Due to the inconsistency in ball feel, predicated upon the shrinking and swelling of your thumb and/or fingers, the only way you can retain a "consistent feel" is through the utilization of tape. There are several types of tape and a variety of procedures to place it in the ball. I will attempt to show you the most functional of those available (obviously, in order to use the tape, you must have oversized holes). These are the types of taping accessories that I recommend:

    · Curity White Adhesive (tacky) 1" wide
    · Johnson & Johnson White Adhesive (slick) 1" wide
    · Masters Inserts White Adhesive (pre-cut) 1" wide
    · 3m Plastic Red and Green ¾" wide
    · Thumb Savers Teflon Strips (pre-cut, blue backing) 1" wide

The procedures for placing the above items in the ball are as varied as the people that are implementing them. I will now relate to you one system for taping the thumb hole that I find to be very functional: (see illustrations on page 40)

The thumb hole. The back of the thumb hole is the area where the thumbnail and the knuckle come into contact with the ball surface. I feel this is where you are to use the plastic tape. Place your fingers in the finger holes and begin to insert your thumb into the ball. Mark the top of the hole with a yellow grease pencil depicting the right and left side of the thumb. Place the initial piece of red plastic tape (cut approximately two inches in length), one-fourth to three-eighths of an inch below the edge of the bevel. Each successive piece is to be graduated slightly (one-sixteenth of an inch). After placing three or four pieces in the back of the hole, in this staggered fashion, place a pre-cut one-inch white adhesive strip in the front of the thumb hole directly opposite the red plastic in the back. Now cut one two-inch long piece of red in half, placing the two three-eighths-inch strips down the exposed sides of the ball between the red plastic in the back and the white adhesive in the front. You have now filled the hole with tape, to a point where little or no ball surface is showing. Continue adding red plastic, your base tape, in the prescribed one sixteenth of an inch graduated fashion until you have a very good feel (able to deliver the ball with no fear of hanging up or losing it). You are now ready for the green plastic tape. As you bowl, your thumb will normally shrink; the addition of the green plastic tape, placed over the top of the red base and attached to the one-fourth of an inch to three-eighths of an inch space at the top of the hole, will serve to eliminate this problem. This overlap serves a two-fold purpose: first; it is utilized to further monitor the fit and feel of the ball as the session

Taping A Thumb Hole

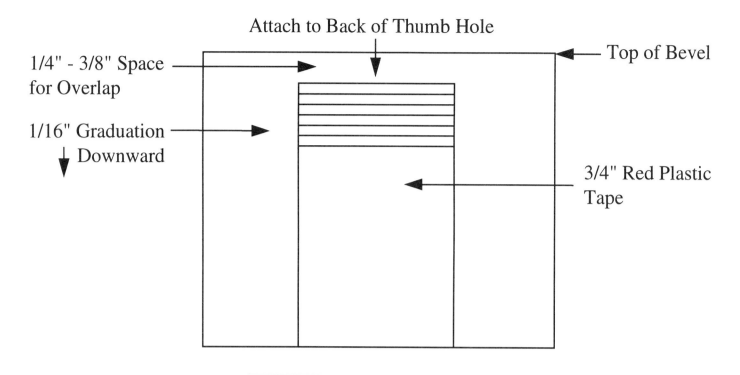

Attach to Back of Thumb Hole

Top of Bevel

1/4" - 3/8" Space
for Overlap

1/16" Graduation
Downward

3/4" Red Plastic
Tape

Green overlap covers the red tape shown to
diminish the ridges created by the graduation.

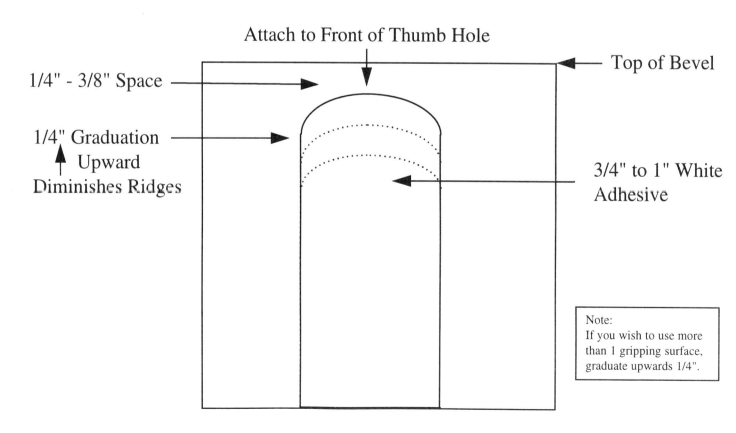

Attach to Front of Thumb Hole

Top of Bevel

1/4" - 3/8" Space

1/4" Graduation
Upward
Diminishes Ridges

3/4" to 1" White
Adhesive

Note:
If you wish to use more
than 1 gripping surface,
graduate upwards 1/4".

progresses and the shrinkage begins and second; it prevents the possibility of the sharp edges of the "graduate red" from causing blisters. Always use a base amount that allows you to place at least one overlap in the hole—preventing any possibility of the edges of the red base coming into play. The purpose of filling the entire hole with tape is so you can take the interior texture of the thumb hole out of play. Some of the reactive resin balls present a very tacky surface; this procedure solves that problem. One point of reference: if you are female, or a small male, you may find that three-fourths of an inch pre-cut adhesive will work better for you because of the smaller circumference of the thumb hole. You may also be required to cut narrower side strips (one fourth of an inch). It is also a possibility that you will prefer the slick adhesive in the front of the thumb hole. I also would like to relate to you that I know a few players that use adhesive in the front and back of the thumb hole. I do not recommend this practice because I feel the thickness of the adhesive versus the thickness of the plastic makes it much harder to control the feel from shot to shot. However, "If it ain't broke, don't fix it." Simply stated: if it works for you, that is all that matters. At the end of each session, remove the overlap and check to see if any base has been removed (this is the reason for the two colors). If any was removed, replace it after cleaning the entire thumb hole with lighter fluid or alcohol. If you do not use this procedure of daily removal and cleaning, a gummy residue will develop. I find that the base amount will vary from as few as three pieces to as many as ten pieces—not including the overlap. Consequently, I recommend that you drill any new equipment when you are "swollen" (thumb is at, or near, its largest size). Remember: a correctly fitted and taped bowling ball will hang onto **you**; you will not have to hang onto **it**. The centrifugal force should pull the ball off your hand at the same point on every shot. A surefire way to determine that a ball is drilled and/or "worked out" incorrectly is to be placed in a situation where if you add one piece of plastic you "hang" and when you remove that piece you "lose it". A correctly implemented and appropriately monitored taping procedure is the only way you can assure yourself of having an opportunity of competing at the highest level possible.

The finger holes. Obviously, the same taping procedure used for the thumb hole would work very nicely for the finger holes. However, since ninety-nine percent of the players that I know use grips, I would like to address another system of controlling the feel in the fingers. I recommend the use of a procedure that requires your ball driller to drill the holes, then ream them slightly, gluing the grips front and back or side to side but not both. This gluing and drilling method will allow you to monitor the shrinking and swelling through the use of one-fourth-inch strips, three-fourths of an inch long, cut from a matchbook; that's right, an ordinary matchbook cover. Tear off the cover from a book of matches and cut it into several strips at the prescribed width and length. When the holes begin to feel loose, insert, with the aid of a thin-blade pocketknife, one or more of the strips on either side between the grip and the surface of the hole. Take care to insure that no part of the matchbook strip is protruding above the surface of the ball as that is a breach of the rules. This process will enable you to control the variations in the fingers caused by shrinkage or swelling.

- **Treating blisters and swelling.** There are three steps to follow:

  1. **The potato.** Believe it or not, this vegetable can do remarkable things where swelling and/or blistering of a finger or thumb is concerned. You simply take an ordinary spud, create an opening large enough for the digit in question, and insert it into the potato. The iodine content of a potato is very high; consequently, it has antiseptic qualities. Also, the compression created by forcing your digit into the spud causes shrinkage. The whole process takes less than thirty minutes, and you essentially, "kill two birds with one spud, uh, stone."

  2. **Dressing the wound.** The results produced by the potato may allow you to proceed with your bowling; however, the open wound will cause you a great deal of anguish. This pain can be somewhat alleviated by utilizing the following procedure:

     a. Puncture the blister, removing all liquid.
     b. Use fingernail clippers to remove all the loose skin around the damaged area.
     c. Place Mentholatum Deep Heat Rub on the open wound; allowing it to remain for one hour.
     d. Wash the wound with hot water and soap.
     e. Dry thoroughly, then place mercurochrome or iodine on the wound.
     f. After two to three hours you can "patch" (nu-skin or cut-patch).

  3. **Protecting the damaged area.** Adhering to the aforementioned procedure will allow you to play the following day. If the pain persists, you must eliminate the friction to the damaged area. Dampen the afflicted area; then rub a yellow grease pencil over it until a substantial yellow residue covers the wound. Place the damaged digit into the ball, then quickly remove it; this should leave a yellow mark at the high friction zone inside the ball. Mark the top of the hole indicating where to insert a thumb saver (teflon-coated strip, cut to the appropriate width). Wash the digit with hot water and soap. Clean the interior of the hole with lighter fluid or alcohol. Place the thumb saver in the proper position thereby eliminating ninety-nine percent of the friction in that area. This procedure will require you to use a tighter hole than normal because of the extremely quick exit created by the insertion of the teflon. I know of a few touring players whose careers were saved by this trick of the trade.

- **Charting the lanes.** Charting is a trick of the trade that can produce an enormous advantage if implemented properly. You simply keep a notebook[3] and list, across the top of the page and/or in the margin, the following information: stance, target, leave,

---

[3]If you would like to own a charting notebook (all necessary information pre-printed), call:(408)374-3340, or write to M & W Products, 985 Hacienda, Campbell, CA 95008.

move, arc, ball in use, mode of adjustment (PAP, ZAP, PZA), time, day, and the establishment in which you are competing. When you find it necessary to make a move, notate the adjustment updating that which is required.

Example:

Date: __6/6/89__   Time: __6 p.m.__   Location: __Carter Lanes Miami, Fla__
Lane: __5__   Ball: __Green Quantum__

Stance	Target	Leave	Move	Arc	ZAP Mode
24	10	Nose	2+1←	7	Zonal or Abstract Left
26	11	Bucket	1+1→	7	Parallel Right
25	10	X	0	6	

Lane: __6__

Stance	Target	Leave	Move	Arc	ZAP Mode
24	10	Brooklyn	4+2←	7	Zonal or Abstract Left
28	12	3,6,9	3+1½←	7	Parallel Right
31	13½	Bucket	1+1→	7	
30	12½	X	0	6	

Note: Examples are for right-handers; if left-handed, simply transpose.

As you can see from this chart, the arc point and equipment were the same; however, there is a 5 & 2½ difference between the 2 lanes (deeper approach and target position on lane 6 versus lane 5). This is the exact type of information that can be invaluable to you. If you draw this pair in the finals, and your opponent is not charting, by the time that person figures out the differential, the match will be over.

I collected four shoeboxes full of 3 by 5 notebooks during my career depicting every bowling center I ever visited. The information in those notebooks is one of the main reasons that a man with severe physical disabilities was able to be competitive, on ocassion, with some of the finest players in the world. When I first introduced charting to many of my professional students, they were reluctant to implement the program because they felt it took too much time and could promote confusion. Eventually, through practicing the method in leagues and during their work-out sessions, they became more adept. Once you are comfortable with the system, you will find that you can, under pressure, do it in your head. Committing it to memory will enable you to make a shot, make the moves, and make the next shot. Then, while your opponent is bowling, you can adjust your charts accordingly.

Remember, differentials from lane to lane are based upon the *surface density*, as well as the maintenance procedures (width, length, viscosity, concentration, etc.). If the surface integrity is upheld, the differentials may remain constant, even if the oiling procedure is

43

altered. If the charts from the previous day make no sense in relation to the current environment, you are back to square one. However, if they depict something close to what you are playing on, you have *created an edge* which is necessary if you would like to have an opportunity to win. If it is not already an integral part, I strongly suggest that you add *charting the lanes* to your repetoire.

I hope that this chapter has increased the size of your personal bag of tricks. If there is anything that you would like to discuss, that was not understood, in this manual, please call this number: **(408) 374-3340**. I'm sure we can find a solution to your particular dilemma.

EPILOGUE

Bowling is one of the most difficult sports in the world to master. Your primary objective is to knock down ten pins; unfortunately, the path your ball must travel is comprised of many hazards most of which are not readily detectable. Your adversaries are not impressed by your size, strength, or intelligence. They never ask any quarter, and, most certainly, never give any. Moreover, they will accept your dedication to perfection by intermittently rewarding you with the ulitimate in imperfection. Your great shots will not always strike; and your bad shots will normally result in nothing short of disaster. Bowling is hard to live with; yet, for most of us, it is impossible to live without. Consequently, the love affair with this terribly demanding and increasingly frustrating game may last forever!